Welcome to Your Journey!

I appreciate your commitment to improving your well-being. This book is designed to equip you with the tools and insights you need to navigate life's challenges with greater flexibility and purpose.

If you have any questions or need further support, please feel free to reach out through my website or email.

AF490044

Unni Babu

Certified CBT and ACT Practitioner

www.unnibabu.com | unniquemind@outlook.com

Preface

To the reader,

Throughout my journey, I have found myself as a listener to countless problems and a witness to the struggles of those seeking solace. It has often been my desire to ease the sorrow of those who come to me with their burdens. I have seen firsthand that serious issues cannot be resolved with a mere phone call or a brief word of encouragement.

This realization has inspired me to create something meaningful—a book that serves as a loyal little companion for those seeking guidance through challenging times. This book is not a cure-all for severe psychological challenges, but rather a gentle guide toward the best life you deserve. Within these pages, you will find tools to help restructure your thoughts, discover what truly matters in life, appreciate the present moment, and acknowledge aspects of yourself that may have been overlooked.

I have purposefully avoided technical jargon that often distances readers from the joy of learning. Much like how seven colors combine to paint the world in brilliant hues, the seven chapters of this book are designed to illuminate your path and guide you toward a brighter, more fulfilling life. Imagine reading this book as if engaging in a heartfelt conversation with a trusted friend—someone who walks alongside you, offering support and insight.

Let us walk this path together.

~ Unni

Contents

Chapter 1

Confront Your Thoughts

"Belief can move mountains" — this idiom beautifully captures the incredible power of belief. I have witnessed and experienced a different, yet equally striking version: **a flawed belief can transform a swift, unstoppable person into an immovable mountain, held captive as a prisoner**. To know how, we must know from where it begins. It begins from thoughts!

You may have already encountered numerous books and sayings that emphasize the profound power of thoughts. Motivational speeches, advertisements... everything bombards us with phrases like "Thought is everything" and "Thoughts decide destiny," so much so that it has become a cliché to say that thoughts determine your life. However, this cliché is too significant a fact to ignore. Thoughts are the invisible architects of our reality, shaping everything we perceive and experience. Our world is a reflection of the thoughts we hold, and every tangible outcome originates from this intangible source. Consider the profound impact of (Ah, a cliché example!) Sir Isaac Newton's moment of curiosity when he wondered why an apple fell downwards instead of upwards. This seemingly simple thought changed our understanding of gravity and propelled scientific advancements, leading to the development of technologies like rockets and satellites. Just as Newton's curious mind was able to reach massive progress, our everyday thoughts hold the potential to transform our lives and the lives of people around us.

The best example to illustrate how a thought can change our lives is an avalanche. A tiny snowflake initiates the process, gathering more snow and gradually increasing in size and impact. Similarly, a single thought gradually gains strength and transforms into a belief, which, over time, increases in intensity and influence over our lives.

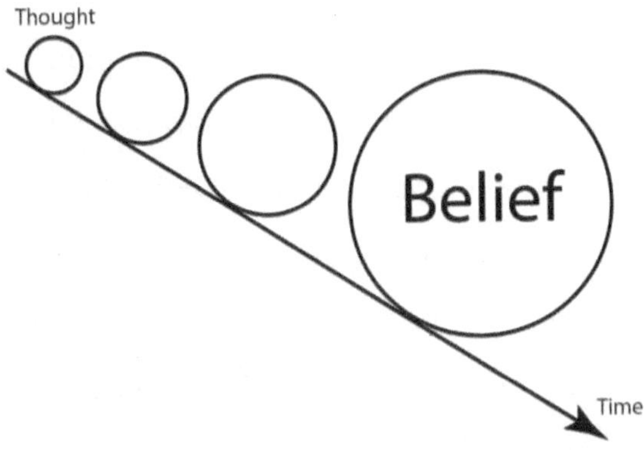

So, thoughts form patterns, which later become beliefs. These beliefs then start to influence our actions and overall perspective on our career, relationships, and other significant domains of life.

CASE 1: *AB is a 32-year-old graphic designer who works from home. Despite her talent and success in her career, AB has always struggled with social interactions. She often feels that nobody likes her and tends to avoid people as a result.*

In this case, the belief "NOBODY LIKES ME," which likely formed from past thoughts influenced by awkward moments and rejections AB may have experienced. These situations, though possibly not as severe as she perceived, contributed to the development of this belief. Her perception of past events and interactions might have been distorted, leading her to internalize this negative belief. As a result, AB's belief has constructed a nearly impenetrable fortress around her mindset. This fortress only allows in information and experiences that reinforce her belief, while dismissing or disregarding anything that contradicts it.

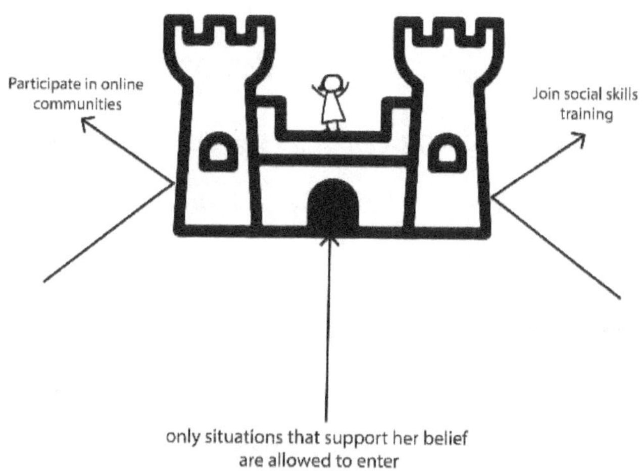

CASE 2: TL is a 16-year-old high school student who excels in most of his subjects but struggles with mathematics. His core belief is "I AM TOO STUPID TO LEARN MATH," which has significantly affected his academic performance and self-esteem.

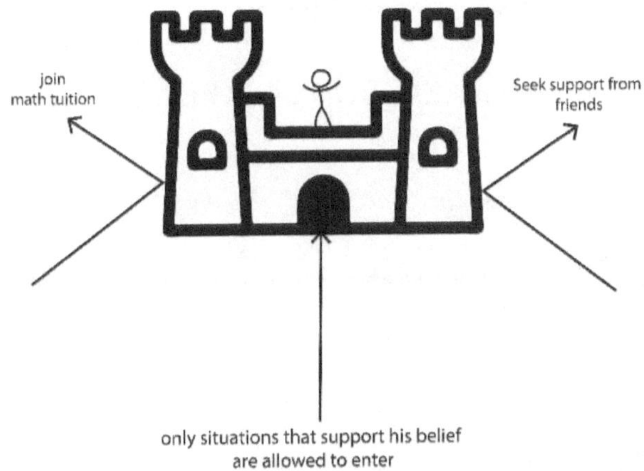

TL might have failed in a maths exam in the past, which may have triggered a negative thought, which later led to the belief "I am too stupid to learn math."

Once thoughts form a belief, it becomes very difficult for a person to change it. Just as it is better to prevent an avalanche by stabilizing the snowpack with methods like planting trees or installing snow fences, it is also better to address and manage thoughts on a daily basis using thought diary. This should become an essential habit, just like brushing, bathing and exercising.

The following illustrates how a more realistic and restructured thought would be:

Negative thought: "NOBODY LIKES ME"

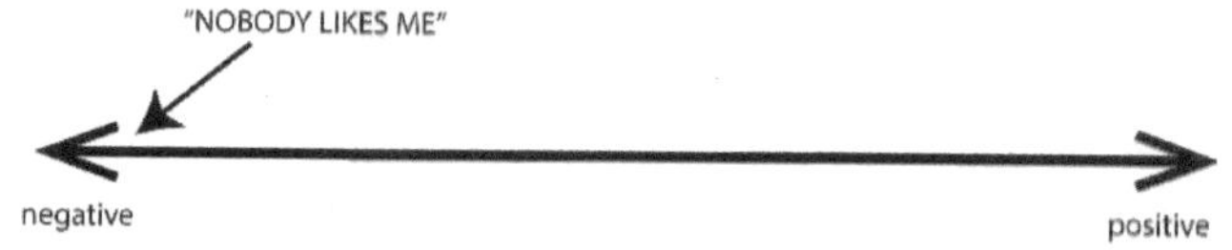

The goal is to shift this extreme negative irrational thought towards positive. But not to shift towards extreme positive side such as

Positive thought: "EVERYBODY LIKES ME"

Because too much of positive is also not aligned with reality and brings trouble too. Hence the goal is to shift it neither too negative nor too unrealistically positive. The following is the desired and realistic thought:

Restructured thought: ""Some people like me, and some people don't. It's natural to have a mix of relationships and opinions from others."

The following table is a template for a thought diary. There are various versions used in different therapies, mainly in CBT, which are more elaborate. The goal is to confront your thoughts—often spontaneous and uninvited—that influence our perceptions and actions, and to restructure them. In other words, a thought diary helps you to shift from spontaneous, irrational, or painful thoughts to more realistic and balanced perspectives.

Date and time	Situation	Thought	What are the reasons that support this thought?	What are the reasons that do not support this thought?	New thought

Column 1. Date and Time: Note when you had a particular negative thought. You may also include the location if needed.

Column 2. Situation: What was the situation that triggered this particular thought?

Column 3. Thought: Write down the thought you had. This column usually contains thoughts that affect you negatively.

Column 4. What are the reasons that support this thought: Here, list the reasons that support your thought with evidence.

Column 5. What are the reasons that do not support this thought: Here, list the reasons that counter the thought and why it may not be valid.

Column 6. New Thought: This is the restructured thought, presenting a more balanced and realistic perspective.

A sample page from my own thought diary is given below for better understanding:

Date and time	Situation	Thought	Reasons that support this thought	Reasons that do not support this thought	New thought
02/03/2024 10:00am	Got less marks in cognitive psychology subject.	*"I am not smart"*	I could not get the marks I wanted. I've had difficulty understanding some concepts.	I had health issues during exam time. I have good marks in more difficult subjects.	*A single exam mark doesn't define my intelligence. I have strengths and potential in other areas too.*
05/15/2024 4:00pm	A close friend didn't acknowledge me when I met him on the street	*"My friend doesn't value our friendship"*	He didn't acknowledge me, which feels like a lack of interest or respect.	He might have been distracted or preoccupied. I have seen him being attentive and caring in other interactions.	*My friend might have been distracted, and this one incident doesn't define the value of our friendship.*

Hence confronting your thoughts is an essential step towards personal growth and mental well-being. By recognizing and challenging irrational or negative thoughts, you can reshape your beliefs to be more balanced and realistic. Just as a single thought can snowball into a powerful belief influencing your actions and outlook, so too can a positive, realistic mindset lead to lasting changes in your life.

Through the use of tools like thought diary, you can gain the ability to identify harmful thinking patterns and replace them with healthier, more empowering perspectives. This process not only enhances your self-esteem but also improves your relationships, career performance, and overall quality of life.

Types of Thoughts You Should Be Aware Of

Certain types of thoughts, if not confronted and restructured, can lead to a miserable life. In cognitive behavior therapy (CBT), these are known as cognitive distortions. Some of them are:

1) This or That Thinking

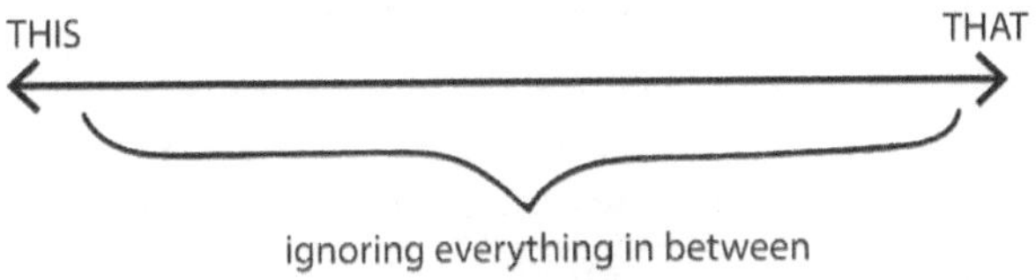

Also called all-or-nothing or dichotomous thinking or black and white thinking. In this type of thinking, situations and outcomes are viewed in black-and-white terms, with no middle ground or shades of gray. This rigid perspective rejects the fact that there are countless shades in most situations.

Examples:

A psychology school student, Sabeena, has just received her exam results. She scored an 85%. However, Sabeena thinks, "<u>If I don't get a perfect score of 100%, I am a complete failure</u>." This thought pattern neglects her achievements and efforts, focusing only on the absence of perfection.

Simran has been dating her partner, Raj, for a year. They recently had a disagreement about their future plans. Simran thinks, "<u>If Raj doesn't agree with me on everything, then he doesn't love me at all</u>." Simran's rigid perspective might cause unnecessary conflict, ignoring the overall love and support they share.

2) Emotional Reasoning

Emotional reasoning involves believing that something is true simply because it feels true, regardless of evidence to the contrary. This thinking associates emotions with facts, leading to distorted interpretations of reality.

Examples:

Jerin feels anxious about an upcoming presentation at college. He thinks, "I feel so nervous, so I must be terrible at public speaking." Despite previous successful presentations and positive feedback from classmates and teachers, Jerin's emotional reasoning convinces him that his nervousness is an indication of incompetence. This distortion ignores objective evidence of his capabilities.

3) Labeling

Labeling involves assigning a fixed label to oneself or others based on a single event or behavior, without considering the evidence. This reduces individuals to false labels.

Example:

After forgetting to submit a report on time, Pravitha thinks, "I'm such an idiot." This label ignores the fact that Pravitha usually meets deadlines and performs well at work. By labeling herself based on one mistake, she ignores her overall competence and *achievements. Similarly, if Pravitha's colleague, Sneha, makes a mistake, she thinks, "<u>She's so careless</u>," ignoring Sneha''s usual diligence and effort.*

4) Magnification and Minimization

Magnification involves magnifying the negatives of oneself or others, while minimization involves downplaying the positives. This leads to a false perception of reality, often resulting in feelings of inadequacy or criticism.

Magnifying
negative

<u>Minimization</u>

Example:

Mercy recently gave a presentation at work. During the presentation, she made a slight mistake while explaining a slide. She thinks, "<u>I made such a big mistake; I might lose my job over this.</u>" Despite the overall success of her presentation, Mercy magnifies *her minor error, believing it could have severe consequences.*

Later, when Mercy receives a promotion, she thinks, "It's just luck; I don't really deserve it." By minimizing her hard work and achievements, Mercy fails to acknowledge her competence and the positive recognition from her superiors.

5) Personalization

Personalization involves believing that others are behaving negatively because of something you did, even when there is no evidence to support this belief. This can lead to unnecessary guilt and self-blame.

Example:

Unni notices that his classmate, Hazeena, seems unusually quiet and distant recently. Unni immediately thinks, "Hazeena must be upset with me; I must have done something wrong." Despite having no reason to believe he is the cause of Hazeena's behavior, Unni personalizes the situation and assumes responsibility. In reality, Hazeena might be dealing with personal issues or simply having a bad day, but Unni's personalization leads him to feel guilty and anxious, impacting him negatively.

6) Tunnel Vision

Seeing only the negatives and ignoring the positives of a situation.

Example:

Nuby is excited for a weekend trip with her family and friends to a lovely hill station. But when she arrives, she notices the hotel room isn't as nice as she expected. Nuby starts thinking, "This trip is going to be a disaster. The room isn't perfect, so everything else will probably go wrong too." By focusing only on the negative aspect, Nuby misses out on enjoying the beautiful scenery and having fun on the trip.

So, the above thoughts are examples of some negative types of thinking you should be aware of. Remember, changing deep-rooted beliefs is not an overnight process, but with consistent effort and practice, it is entirely achievable. Embrace the journey of confronting your thoughts as an ongoing practice of self-awareness and self-improvement. By doing so, you take control of your life, paving the way for a more fulfilling and harmonious life.

Let the fortress built by flawed beliefs crumble, and let life bring you more rewarding experiences.

Chapter 2
Metaphors – See Beyond the Horizon

"The greatest thing by far is to be a master of metaphor."

~ Aristotle

A villager shouted, "The shadow of a striped storm arrives from the horizon!" Nobody could fully understand what he said and they continued their work until they saw a tiger approaching them. It was then they realized that using direct, concrete language is crucial for survival. When faced with real threats, clarity and precision are key. However, in the psychological realm, it is not always possible to rely solely on direct, concrete language. Here, everything is intangible, and abstract language becomes a powerful tool. Some experiences and emotions are too complex to be neatly packaged into straightforward words. They dodge direct descriptions, slipping through the cracks of literal language.

Abstract language, through the use of metaphors and other figurative expressions, provides a way to bridge this gap. It allows us to convey a picture of our inner world, offering a richer understanding. For instance, saying someone feels "like a ship lost at sea" paints a vivid picture of their sense of aimlessness and isolation in a way that simply saying "they feel lost" cannot. This chapter explores how metaphors can enhance our psychological well-being. By transforming the abstract into relatable, metaphors not only help us express our own feelings but also enable others to understand us more deeply. In the psychological realm, metaphors are more than just a "show-off" of your language skills — they are indispensable tools for communication and healing.

Metaphors are powerful tools for conveying deep insights and truths about our experiences and perceptions. The metaphors in this context is not for your English literature exam, the metaphors we use here are to describe the self (YOU). They are designed to highlight the unwavering and constant nature of your true self, even amidst life's chaos and challenges.

Imagine yourself as the calm in the middle of a tornado. The tornado represents the countless external pressures, stressors, and emotional disturbances you might encounter. However, at the center of this tornado (eye of the tornado), there is a place of stillness—this is your true self. No matter how turbulent the tornado gets, this calm center remains unaffected, a constant presence within you.

These metaphors serve a dual purpose: they bring clarity to your mind and provide a deeper understanding of your true self. They remind you that, despite the external circumstances, your self exists as an unchanging, constant truth. This realization can be grounding and empowering, helping you navigate through life's storms with a sense of peace and stability.

For example, consider the metaphor of a lighthouse. In the face of raging seas and dark skies (your thoughts and external situations), the lighthouse (YOU) stands firm. This lighthouse represents your true self—firm and reliable, guiding you safely through the turbulent waters of life. The light it emits is your inner wisdom and strength, illuminating your path even when everything around you seems chaotic.

Another metaphor could be that of a mountain. No matter how fierce the winds or how heavy the rains (your thoughts and external situations), the mountain (YOU) stands tall and unyielding. Its strength and stability are a reflection of your true self, enduring and constant, unaffected by the changing weather. This metaphor can help you remember that, like the mountain, you have an inner strength that remains steadfast regardless of external conditions.

Using such metaphors can deepen your understanding of the self and reinforce the truth that, despite any storms you face, your true self remains a calm, unchanging presence. The metaphors above serve as powerful reminders of several crucial insights about our relationship with thoughts and the nature of the self. They help us realize the following:

1. **Do Not Cling to Your Thoughts:** The metaphors of the calm in the middle of a tornado, the lighthouse, and the mountain illustrate the importance of not clinging to thoughts that can cause psychological issues. Just as the calm center of the tornado remains unaffected by the

swirling chaos around it, you too can learn to observe your thoughts without getting caught up in them. By recognizing that thoughts are temporary and ever-changing, you can avoid becoming overwhelmed by them and reduce their impact on your mental well-being.

2. **Maintain Distance between Yourself and Your Thoughts:** These metaphors encourage you to maintain a healthy distance between yourself and your thoughts. By seeing yourself as the calm center or the lighthouse, you adopt a non-judgmental approach to your thoughts. This detachment allows you to observe your thoughts without identifying with them, bringing greater clarity and perspective to your mind. It's like watching the storm from a place of safety and calm, rather than being swept away by it.

3. **Recognize the Changing Nature of Thoughts:** The metaphors highlight the short-lived nature of thoughts compared to the constancy of the self. Thoughts, like the storm or the raging seas, are always in flux, coming and going. However, your

true self, represented by the calm center, the lighthouse, or the mountain, remains constant and unchanging. This understanding helps you see that while thoughts may be disruptive, they do not define you. Your true self is a stable foundation, unaffected by the turbulence of your thoughts.

4. **Evoke Emotions and Bring Clarity:** Metaphors have the unique ability to evoke emotions and bring clarity simultaneously. They paint vivid pictures that resonate on an emotional level, making abstract concepts more tangible and relatable. By visualising yourself as the calm center of a tornado or the lighthouse, you can tap into a sense of inner peace and strength. These images not only clarify the nature of the self but also inspire a sense of stability in the middle of life's challenges.

Including these metaphors into your daily reflections can profoundly impact your mental and emotional well-being. They remind you to let go of the thoughts that cause distress, maintain a non-judgmental distance from your thoughts, and recognize the enduring constancy of your true self. Through these vivid and emotionally resonant images, you can cultivate a deeper understanding of yourself and navigate life's storms with greater ease and clarity.

Metaphors are powerful tools used in various psychotherapies, particularly in Acceptance and Commitment Therapy (ACT). In ACT, metaphors help individuals understand and relate to their experiences in a more meaningful way, facilitating psychological flexibility and acceptance of thoughts and feelings.

Beyond psychotherapy, metaphors are integral to spiritual practices, such as Buddhism. In Buddhism, monks often contemplate the profound truths of life through metaphors, which serve as gateways to deeper understanding and enlightenment. Zen Buddhists, in particular, use metaphors known as Zen Koans. These Koans are paradoxical statements or questions that challenge conventional thinking, leading to insights and awakening.

The metaphors mentioned above are popular ones used in ACT. However, true understanding and learning occur when you create and contemplate metaphors based on your personal experiences. Such metaphors add a unique, individualized perspective, making them more meaningful and relevant to your journey. I have developed some metaphors related to my own understanding of the self and my thoughts. Here are a few of the metaphors I have created on my way from college to my home:

- ❖ *I am standing near the zebra crossing by my college at IGNOU, Kochi. I see vehicles rushing left and right, like my thoughts. Yet, I am not attached to any of them. Slowly, they move away, paving the way for a clear path forward for me to cross. If I had clung to any vehicle, obsessing over a Benz, BMW, or Audi, I would not see the clear gap for me to cross.*

- ❖ *I am on the bus heading towards my home in Koothattukulam town. Sitting on the side seat, I gaze at the sky. Clouds of different shades of grey pass by, much like my thoughts. Yet, the sky doesn't cling to any of them and remains clear and clean, just like the self.*

❖ *The bus I am on is one among many that reach the bus stop. Just like buses that arrive and depart from the bus station, my thoughts come and go. The self is the bus stop, observing the comings and goings without getting carried away by any particular bus.*

❖ *I reach home and turn on my laptop. The screen displays movies - horror movies mirroring my deepest fears, feel-good movies reflecting moments of joy. The speakers sing a symphony of emotions - mournful songs echoing sadness, upbeat tunes echoing happiness. Yet, through it all, the laptop itself remains unchanged. It simply presents the content, without getting swept away by the emotions on display. Just like the laptop, I am the constant observer of my thoughts and feelings. They may be positive or negative,*

In Chapter 1, you learned to reframe your thoughts into more positive and realistic versions. In this chapter, you have learned to distance yourself from your thoughts and focus on what truly matters using the power of metaphors. By combining two key strategies —reframing and distancing from thoughts—you can bring about tremendous change in your life when practiced effectively.

Chapter 3

Values – Live Your Life, Not Theirs

"Strive not to be a success, but rather to be of value."

~ Albert Einstein

What I love about art is that its soul lies in expression. It does not have an inherent goal or destination. There is no right or wrong, just like how one person might prefer mango ice cream while another prefers chocolate ice cream. It would be awkward to ask if selecting mango ice cream is right instead of the other because it is a personal preference. Similarly, if we ask a kid why he is playing with blocks instead of reading a quantum physics book, the kid would be confused. What the kid does aligns with what gives him joy.

These examples point us to a fundamental truth about life: it should not be lived based on the blueprint set by others and their preferences. Instead, life should be lived according to individual preferences that are guided by an invisible force called values. Living according to values means making choices and taking actions that resonate with our true selves, rather than conforming to external expectations.

Once upon a time in a far-off land, there was a renowned healer celebrated by everyone for his miraculous abilities. He had healed countless people, including the King himself, and lived a prosperous life filled with admiration. However, on his deathbed, despite all his success, he was both sad and a bit angry.

As he lay there, surrounded by well-wishers, he shouted with a mix of frustration and regret, "I spent my entire life as a healer because my parents forced me to follow the path that promised wealth and respect. But what I truly wanted was to be a warrior!"

In the above example, the healer valued saving lives and excelled in that aspect throughout his life. However, his own values of fighting, courage, winning battles, and a passion for weapons remained unfulfilled. These desires were overshadowed by the burden of living up to the values imposed by his parents since childhood.

What you see in existence is the interplay of duality: Day gives way to night, the masculine complements the feminine, and life precedes death. This concept of duality extends throughout existence. However, values transcend this binary realm, especially of the duality of right and wrong.

Issues
- Increased stress and anxiety
- Depression
- A sense of emptiness or lack of purpose
- Increased risk of physical health problems
- Reduced energy levels

Values operate on a higher plane, serving as your North Pole star, which is only seen by you, guiding you towards what truly matters in life. They are not simply a matter of morality, but rather an intrinsic part of yourself. Your values provide the strength and direction to pursue our deepest desires, those which may lie hidden within the unconscious. A life lived without a strong foundation of values is ultimately an unfulfilled one. When you live according to your values, you find greater fulfillment and authenticity in your life. They provide a sense of direction and purpose, allowing you to navigate the complexities of life with clarity and confidence.

<u>Values — Always Within Your Sight</u>

Values are always within sight and can be acted upon immediately, which is why I represented them as a star in the illustration in previous page.

Imagine your value is creativity—this means you can begin a creative activity right now, like sketching, writing, or brainstorming new ideas. If your value is health, you can take a moment to support it by doing a quick workout, enjoying a piece of fruit, or taking a short walk. The essence of values is that they are not abstract concepts waiting for a future time; instead, they are practical and actionable in the present moment. They guide your actions and decisions in real-time, helping you align with what truly matters to you. By tapping into your values, you can make choices that reflect your true priorities and enhance your sense of fulfillment, making the star a fitting symbol for how values shine brightly and guide you throughout your day.

Finding Your Values

Finding values is an essential part of many psychotherapies. It is only through identifying and understanding your core values that you can lay out a plan for a better life. Discovering your values is not as challenging as finding your soul mate. All it takes is patience, self-understanding, and a piece of paper and a pen.

Think about the values that are important to you. Note them down on a piece of paper like the one shown below:

MY VALUES

Adventure

Courage

Freedom

Humour

Beauty

Creativity

Love

Gratitude

Health

For example, I wrote "beauty" in my list of values. This means I find, value, enjoy, and appreciate beauty in various aspects of life: in creative works, in the appearance and fashion of some people, in nature, etc. Whenever I buy a phone, my tech-savvy friends recommend phones with good specifications such as a good camera, processor, memory, and so on. While I consider such specifications, I also value the beauty in things I buy. Hence, I consider the User Interface (default themes, icons) a significant factor in purchasing a phone because it is the user interface that I am constantly interacting with. This is why companies invest millions in improving the aesthetics of a product—for those who value beauty.

Now, your values might be entirely different. Write them down and then rank which are the values that you cannot live without. These values will be your core values. Core values must always be followed, or else you will face regret and dissatisfaction later in life. Core values act as a compass, guiding your decisions and actions, ensuring that you live a life that is true to yourself and aligned with what matters most to you.

Prioritizing Your Values

Imagine someone trapped in an abusive relationship. This person deeply values love, freedom, and self-care. However, the abusive relationship is causing immense suffering, overshadowing their ability to live in alignment with their core values. In such a scenario, it's crucial for the person to prioritize self-care and freedom above the value of love. Such situations demand a shift in the prioritization of values.

Understand values to understand others

A major shortcoming in a person is the failure to understand the importance of values. Many people, even in late adulthood, struggle to grasp that values are subjective. This lack of understanding creates a distance between them and others, particularly with younger generations. The values of one generation are often different from those of another, and even within the same generation, individual values can vary greatly.

Realizing that values are subjective and that there is no absolute right or wrong can lead to a deeper understanding of oneself and others. This awareness fosters a broader mindset and smoother interpersonal relationships. When you acknowledge that others' values are just as valid as your own, you become more open-minded and empathetic. This understanding helps bridge generational gaps and enhances connections with people who may have different perspectives and priorities.

Ultimately, appreciating the subjectivity of values allows you to navigate social interactions with greater ease and respect, leading to more harmonious and fulfilling relationships.

<u>A sample scenario:</u>

Mr. J: A 45-year-old man who values financial stability and practicality.

Ms. L: A 35-year-old woman who values creativity and artistic expression

Mr. J and Ms. L are in a relationship and are discussing their plans for the future. They are sitting in their living room, surrounded by a mix of practical and Ms. L's art pieces furniture (more like mute spectators in coliseum).

Mr. J: "Ms. L, I've been thinking. We need to start saving more for our future. I was looking at our expenses, and I think we should cut down on some of the non-essential stuff."

Ms. L: "What do you mean by non-essential?"

Mr. J: "Like your art supplies and those painting classes you take. We could save a lot if we cut back on those expenses."

Ms. L: "But Mr. J, those classes and supplies are really important to me. They help me express myself and unwind after a long day."

Mr. J: "I understand that, but they don't contribute to our financial stability. We need to be practical here. Art won't pay the bills or secure our future."

Ms. L: "Not everything is about money, Mr. J! Art is a part of who I am. It's how I find joy and meaning in life."

Mr. J: "That's just a hobby, Ms. L. We need to prioritize things that are truly important."

Ms. L: "You don't get it, do you? To me, art is not just a hobby. It's a core part of my identity. Just because it's not important to you doesn't mean it's not valuable."

Mr. J: "I'm just trying to be practical. We need to be responsible adults and think about our future."

Ms. L: "And I am thinking about our future. A future where I'm happy and fulfilled, not just financially secure. You need to understand that my values are different from yours. Just because you don't see the value in something doesn't mean it's not there."

Mr. J: "I guess I never really thought about it that way. I've always focused on what makes sense financially."

Ms. L: "And that's okay, but you need to recognize that we have different values. If we want to make this work, we need to respect each other's perspectives."

Mr. J: "You're right. I'm sorry, Ms. L. I didn't mean to dismiss your passion. I'll try to understand your point of view better."

Ms. L: "Thank you, Mr. J. I appreciate that. Let's find a balance that works for both of us."

Understanding and respecting the subjective nature of values is crucial for nurturing harmonious relationships. Just as Mr. J and Ms. L navigated their conflict by recognizing and appreciating each other's values, we too can enhance our interpersonal connections by being open-minded and empathetic. Acknowledging that values differ from person to person, and even across generations, allows us to bridge gaps and develop deeper understanding. By living in alignment with our core values and respecting the values of others, we pave the way for more meaningful and fulfilling relationships. Remember, it's not about finding the right values, but about honouring the ones that resonate deeply with each of us.

Chapter 4

Timetable – Craft the Blueprint of Your Life

"All we have to decide is what to do with the time that is given us."

~ J. R. R. Tolkien

When you are broken, when you are furious, you may break some things, throw some things. But do you gouge your eyes out? Do you chop off your hands? Why? Because even in the midst of heartbreaking moments, you are aware that losing your vision and limbs will later make your life miserable, cause unimaginable suffering later. And even if you were to do something so extreme, the physical pain would immediately remind you of their value.

But the most precious of all, when it is lost, you may not be aware because it doesn't give pain so quickly. What is the most precious thing of all? It is TIME!

Time is your most valuable resource, yet it is often taken for granted. Unlike physical pain, the consequences of wasted time are not immediately felt. However, as days, months, and years pass, the weight of lost opportunities and unfulfilled goals becomes apparent. This delayed realization can lead to deep regret.

Wasting time is often viewed as a sin, one that can lead to deep regret and numerous irreversible losses later in life. The consequences of mismanaging time are not just short-lived; they can accumulate over the years, resulting in missed opportunities, unfulfilled goals, and a diminished quality of life. Therefore, it is crucial to remain vigilant about how you spend your time.

A well-structured timetable serves as a valuable tool in this regard. It acts as a roadmap, helping you delineate between what is essential and what is not.

By planning out your activities, you ensure that you allocate sufficient time to priorities, making it less likely that you'll fall into the trap of procrastination or distraction. This kind of planning helps you maintain focus on your goals and ensures that your efforts are directed toward meaningful and productive endeavors.

It is important to recognize that a timetable is not limited to academic or professional settings. While it is common to use timetables in schools, colleges, and offices to organize work and study schedules, the principle of effective time management extends beyond these environments. Vacations, travel, and leisure activities can also benefit from thoughtful planning. Even during downtime or relaxation periods, having a rough plan can enhance the quality of your experiences and prevent wasted moments.

For instance, when planning a vacation, a timetable can help you make the most of your time by ensuring that you visit all the places you want to see and engage in activities that interest you, rather than spending the trip feeling unorganized or aimless.

Similarly, in leisure time, setting aside moments for hobbies, exercise, or social activities can lead to a more fulfilling and balanced life.

Mr. J's Missed Opportunities in Italy

Mr. J had always dreamed of visiting Italy. When he finally got the opportunity for a two-day tour, he was thrilled. His excitement was intense, and he eagerly anticipated the trip.

However, when Mr. J arrived in Italy, his lack of a detailed plan quickly became apparent. Despite his initial enthusiasm, he hadn't created a timetable for his trip. Instead of having a clear schedule, he found himself repeatedly debating what to do next. Should he visit the Vatican Museums or explore the Tuscan countryside? Should he spend the morning in Venice or the afternoon in Milan? Without a structured plan, he spent a significant amount of time deliberating, rather than experiencing the sights.

As the days passed, Mr. J's indecision led to wasted time and missed opportunities. He found himself frequently looking at his watch, feeling the pressure of unfulfilled plans. Instead of immersing himself in the rich history and vibrant culture of Italy, he was preoccupied with the uncertainty of what to do next.

Upon returning to his office, Mr. J sat at his desk, reflecting on his trip. He opened his computer and looked at the pictures of Italian landmarks that had once filled him with excitement. Now, however, these images stirred feelings of regret and sadness. The grandeur of the Colosseum, the charm of Venice, and the beauty of Florence seemed to mock him, reminding him of the experiences he missed out on.

Mr. J realized that his lack of a proper timetable had reduced the joy of his trip. The excitement that had once filled him was replaced with frustration over the time he had wasted. This experience served as a sad reminder of the importance of planning and time management, even for leisure activities. Moving forward, Mr. J vowed to create detailed schedules for future trips to ensure he could make the most of every moment and avoid the regret of missed opportunities.

We can continue to exist and achieve greatness even if we lose money, people, or even the precious senses and limbs mentioned at the beginning of the chapter. However, we cannot exist without time; therefore, we must respect its value—always and forever. Let this realisation help you create a timetable and make the most of every moment.

Key domains of a daily timetable

A well-structured daily timetable should encompass several key domains to ensure a balanced and fulfilling life. Here's a closer look at each of these domains:

1. Productivity

Productivity involves tasks related to work, studies, or any other goal-oriented activities. This domain should cover your professional responsibilities, academic pursuits, or personal projects. Including specific time blocks for these activities helps you stay organized, meet deadlines, and maintain progress toward your goals. Effective time management in this area ensures that you are not only accomplishing tasks efficiently but also setting aside time for planning and reflection. This might include:

- **Work-related tasks**: Meetings, project work, and administrative duties.

- **Academic studies**: Lectures, study sessions, and research.

- **Personal projects**: Writing, creative endeavors, or skill development.

2. Social Connection

Social Connection refers to the time spent nurturing relationships with family, friends, and colleagues. Building and maintaining these connections is crucial for emotional well-being and can provide support, joy, and a sense of belonging. This domain should include:

- **Family time**: Activities with loved ones, family dinners, or regular check-ins.

- **Friends**: Social gatherings, phone calls, or virtual meetups.

- **Networking**: Professional interactions, mentorship, or community involvement.

3. Physical Activity

Physical Activity involves activities that promote physical health and well-being. Regular exercise is essential for maintaining physical fitness, reducing stress, and boosting overall health. A balanced timetable should allocate time for:

- **Exercise routines**: Gym workouts, jogging, yoga, or sports activities.

- **Physical chores**: Housework, gardening, or any other physical tasks that contribute to overall activity levels.

- **Health maintenance**: Medical appointments, preventative care, or wellness practices.

4. Leisure

Leisure involves activities that provide relaxation and enjoyment, helping to recharge your mental and emotional batteries. Including leisure time into your schedule ensures that you have opportunities for rest, creativity, and personal satisfaction. This domain can include:

- **Hobbies**: Reading, crafting, cooking, or any activity that brings joy.

- **Entertainment**: Watching movies, playing games, or attending events.

- **Relaxation**: Meditation, walking, or simply unwinding after a busy day.

By integrating the above mentioned domains into your daily timetable, you create a balanced structure that supports productivity, fosters relationships, promotes physical health, and provides space for relaxation and enjoyment. A well-rounded approach to time management helps ensure that you lead a fulfilling and well-balanced life, addressing all aspects of your well-being.

As I discussed in the previous chapter about the importance of values, it's essential to incorporate activities that reflect your core values into your daily timetable. Specifically, I emphasized four domains—productivity, social connection, physical work or exercise, and leisure—because each plays a critical role in your overall well-being. Here's why these domains are important and the consequences of neglecting them:

Lack of productivity can lead to a host of negative outcomes. When productivity is low or absent, you might experience increased stress due to a backlog of tasks and unmet deadlines. This stress can worsen feelings of anxiety and decrease overall life satisfaction. Additionally, missing deadlines and failing to achieve goals often result in lost opportunities for career advancement or personal growth. Persistent lack of productivity can stall career progress and hinder personal achievement. Over time, repeated failures and missed goals can diminish your motivation, creating a cycle where decreased motivation further hampers performance.

Lack of social connection has been linked to significant adverse effects on both mental and physical health. Social isolation can lead to heightened feelings of loneliness and emotional distress, with chronic loneliness being associated with a higher risk of depression, anxiety, and even cardiovascular disease. Strong social connections contribute significantly to overall well-being and happiness. Research consistently shows that robust social networks enhance mental health and increase life satisfaction. Additionally, the absence of social interaction can result in a lack of emotional and practical support during challenging times, which is crucial for coping with stress and maintaining resilience.

Lack of physical work or exercise carries well-documented health risks. Insufficient physical activity can lead to a range of health problems, including obesity, cardiovascular disease, and diabetes. Regular exercise is essential for maintaining physical health and preventing chronic diseases. A sedentary lifestyle not only reduces energy levels but can also lead to increased fatigue. Engaging in regular physical activity enhances overall energy and reduces feelings of tiredness.

Furthermore, exercise has been shown to improve mood and reduce symptoms of depression and anxiety, making it an important component of mental health.

Lack of leisure activities can have several harmful effects on well-being. Without adequate leisure time, individuals may experience burnout and exhaustion. Regular downtime and engaging in enjoyable activities are vital for preventing burnout and maintaining mental health. A lack of leisure can also suppress creativity and problem-solving abilities, as engaging in hobbies and relaxation activities fosters cognitive functioning and creativity. Finally, leisure activities contribute to overall life satisfaction and happiness, with research indicating that individuals who regularly engage in enjoyable activities report higher levels of well-being and satisfaction with their lives.

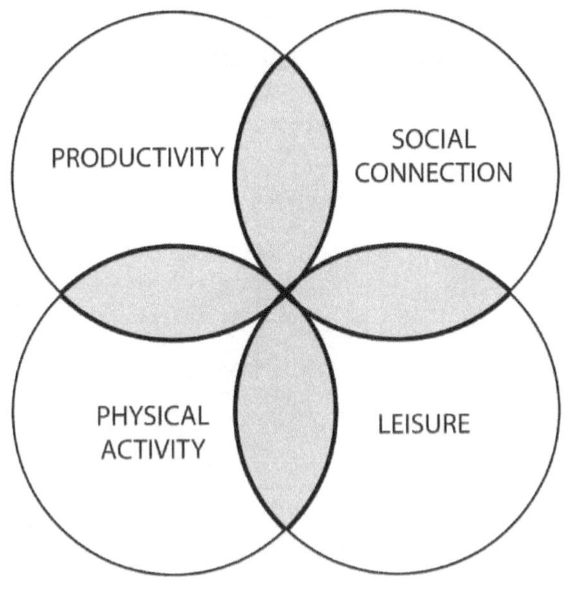

Imagine a flower with four vibrant petals, each representing a crucial domain of your daily timetable: Productivity, Social Connection, Physical Activity, and Leisure. These petals converge harmoniously at the center, symbolizing the balance and fulfillment that comes from nurturing each aspect of your life. Just as a flower needs all its petals to bloom fully, your well-being thrives when you give attention to all these domains. The flower of time is a reminder that a well-rounded life, like a blossoming flower, is both beautiful and essential.

Chapter 5

Goal - Steps Towards Fulfillment

"If you want to live a happy life, tie it to a goal, not to people or objects."

~ Albert Einstein

In the previous chapters, we explored the twin pillars of a fulfilling life: the appreciation of value and the power of time management. We learned how to identify what truly matters and how to structure our days to maximize our potential. But our journey doesn't end there. To truly live a life of purpose and satisfaction, we need to set our sights on something extraordinary: goals.

Imagine your goal as a beloved waiting for you with open arms, a dream prince or princess eager to embrace you. Just as a romantic relationship fills our lives with meaning and excitement, pursuing a goal can ignite a fire within us, propelling us forward with unwavering determination.

The path to achieving our goals is not always smooth or predictable. It may be filled with challenges and even setbacks. But it is this journey that makes life truly worth living. Each step we take brings us closer to our dreams, each obstacle we overcome strengthens our resolve, and each milestone we reach fills us with a sense of accomplishment that is hard to match.

Let us embark on this exciting chapter together, where we will uncover the secrets of goal setting, learn how to craft a roadmap to success, and discover the unwavering motivation that will carry us through every twist and turn. Remember, your dreams are waiting – are you ready to embrace the adventure?

Values and Goals

Values and goals are closely connected, forming the foundation of a fulfilling life. Although they are different in nature, they rely on each other, each providing strength and purpose to the other.

Values act as our moral guide, directing our decisions and actions. Without values, our goals lack a proper direction and may lead us in directions that conflict with our true selves. For instance, if honesty is a core value, the pursuit of financial success should be ethical, without compromising integrity (else it would be sleepless nights and anxious days).

Imagine your values as the soul of your existence, the essence that defines who you are and what you believe in. They are the guiding light that illuminates your path and influences your choices. Without a strong soul, your goals might be like a body without a direction, moving aimlessly and lacking purpose. For instance, if you value compassion but pursue success with ruthless ambition, it's like having a body driven by a soul that isn't in sync with its actions.

Now, think of your goals as the body that gives form and movement to your soul. They bring your values into the real world, turning your values into actions. Goals are the muscles and bones that allow your values to interact with the world, creating meaningful impact. Without goals, your values might remain as abstract ideas, never fully realized, like a soul without a body—full of potential but unable to manifest its true power ☹

Miracle Questioning

Miracle questioning is a powerful technique used to help individuals imagine a desired future. By asking questions that encourage people to imagine a world where their problems have vanished, this approach helps uncover hidden desires, values, and potential goals. It's a tool that shifts focus from problems to possibilities, allowing individuals to create a vision of their ideal life. This technique is used in counselling and therapies like Solution focused therapy, CBT etc.

Imagine a moonlit night where everything is calm and peaceful. Suddenly, you see me, Unni, a wise and mystical figure, appearing before you. With a gentle wave of my hand, I cast a magical spell, and just like that, all your problems have vanished!!

"Welcome," I say warmly, "I'm here to help you uncover your deepest desires and set meaningful goals. Let's start by imagining that your life is

exactly as you want it to be—without any obstacles. What do you see? What are you doing? How does your ideal life look?"

I show you a magical mirror, glowing softly. "Look into this mirror and picture your perfect life," I encourage. "Imagine everything has gone right, and all your problems are gone. What changes do you see? What are you most excited about?"

As you imagine this ideal scenario, think about what's really important to you. What values and goals stand out in this vision?

"Now, write down what you see"

This technique will help you clarify what you truly want for yourself and identify the values you hold dear. You can use this technique to uncover both your own values and goals, as well as to help others who are struggling to find theirs.

<u>SMART</u> Goals

A significant source of disappointment and frustration arises from setting goals that are not

SMART. People often incline towards goals that are either fundamentally misaligned with their personal values. This disagreement between dreams and reality inevitably leads to self-doubt and disillusionment. When goals are detached from our core beliefs or lack concrete parameters, we set ourselves up for failure. It's like building a house on shifting sands. To avoid this risky foundation, goals must stick to a specific framework. This framework is known as SMART (Specific, Measurable, Achievable, Relevant, Time-bound).

S = Specific

If I ask you what your goal is and you respond with something like, "I want to be happy," or "I want to have a good life," these are not specific goals. They lack a clear direction and concrete steps, making them intangible and difficult to achieve. It's like trying to grasp a ghost—there's nothing solid to hold onto.

Specific goals, on the other hand, are well-defined. They provide a clear target to aim for and a roadmap to follow. Specific goals transform abstract desires into concrete plans, giving your efforts purpose and direction. They give your values a tangible form, much like a body that moves and interacts with the world.

For instance, instead of saying, "I want to be happy," you might set a specific goal like, "I want to write a psychology book." This goal is concrete. It breaks down the broad concept of happiness into a specific task that you can work towards.

Similarly, instead of saying, "I want to have a good life," you might set specific goals such as, "I want to master the piano," or "I want to run a marathon," or "I want to start my own business." Each of these goals is precise and achievable, providing a clear path to follow.

M = Measurable

To achieve success, your goals must be measurable. Vague goals like "reaching the ocean's depths" or "touching the sky" are unlikely to be realized due to their lack of specificity and feasibility. Unless used metaphorically, these goals are like measuring the immeasurable.

Measurable goals provide a clear roadmap to success. By tracking your progress, you gain a sense of accomplishment, boosting motivation. This visibility helps you stay focused and committed. Without measurable markers, it's difficult to assess your progress and make necessary adjustments.

Instead of setting abstract goals, focus on those with clear metrics. For instance, "finishing a psychology book by year's end" is measurable with a specific deadline. Similarly, "practicing piano for an hour daily to master three pieces in six months" outlines clear steps and outcomes.

Measurable goals transform abstract dreams into achievable milestones (just like levels in games, or checkpoints in a racing game). They offer a way to monitor progress and celebrate successes, ultimately increasing your chances of reaching your full potential.

A = Achievable

Setting targets that are within reach promotes motivation and perseverance. When goals are attainable, individuals experience a sense of accomplishment as they progress towards their desired outcomes. Conversely, unachievable goals can lead to frustration and discouragement. For example, aiming to become a billionaire overnight is unrealistic and demotivating. A more practical goal would be to increase monthly savings by a specific percentage. By setting achievable targets and breaking down larger goals into smaller steps, individuals can increase their chances of success and build confidence.

R = Relevant

A relevant goal is one that aligns with your overall objectives and values. It should contribute positively to your personal or professional life. When a goal is relevant, it provides a clear sense of purpose and direction.

By setting relevant goals, you focus your energy and resources on what truly matters. This helps you avoid wasting time and effort on pursuits that do not align with your long-term goals. For example, if your career goal is to become a software engineer, learning a foreign language might not be directly relevant at this stage, unless it's required for a specific job opportunity. The goal would be something like learning Java or Python in this scenario.

T = Time-bound

A time-bound goal is one that has a specific deadline. This element is crucial in transforming goals into actionable plans. By setting a clear timeframe, you create a sense of urgency and focus.

When a goal has a deadline, it becomes more tangible and measurable. It helps you prioritize tasks and allocate resources efficiently. For instance, saying "I want to lose weight" is a vague goal. However, stating "I want to lose 10 pounds <u>by the end of the</u>

month" provides a clear target and a sense of direction.

Time-bound goals also enhance motivation. Knowing that you have a specific timeframe to achieve your objective can be a powerful motivator. It encourages you to stay focused and make consistent progress.

Example: About writing a psychology book

Dimension	Not SMART	SMART
Specific	"I want to be successful."	"I will write and publish a 300-page psychology book."
Measurable	"I want to write a book."	"I want to complete and submit my 300-page psychology book manuscript

		by December 31st."
Achievable	"I want to write a 1000-page book in one month."	"I will write 10 pages per week to complete my psychology book by the end of the year."
Relevant	"I want to learn to swim." (not relevant for now, in this context)	"I want to write a psychology book to contribute to my field of expertise."
Time-bound	"I want to finish my book soon."	"I want to have my psychology book completed and published by December 31st."

Combining all the SMART examples for writing a psychology book, my SMART goal will be:

> *"I want to write and publish a 300-page psychology book by December 31st. To achieve this, I will write 10 pages per week, focusing on content relevant to my field. I will complete and submit my manuscript by the end of the year"* (ensuring that the goal is specific, measurable, achievable, relevant, and time-bound)

Now, I'm going to take this goal and write it out on a bright chart paper with colorful pens, making it impossible to ignore. I'll hang it on my wall where I can see it every day, a vibrant reminder of what I'm working toward and why it matters.

Breaking a Goal into sub goals

One effective technique for breaking a goal into manageable sub-goals is to visualize it as a staircase. Here's how it works (widely used in psychotherapies such as CBT):

Step 1) Draw the Staircase

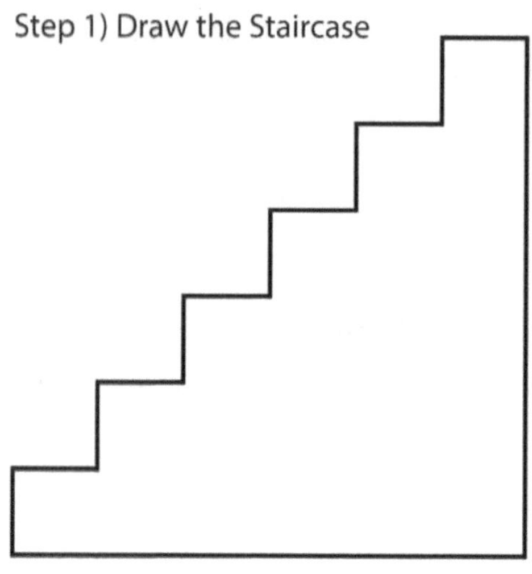

Step 2) Write initial state and goal state

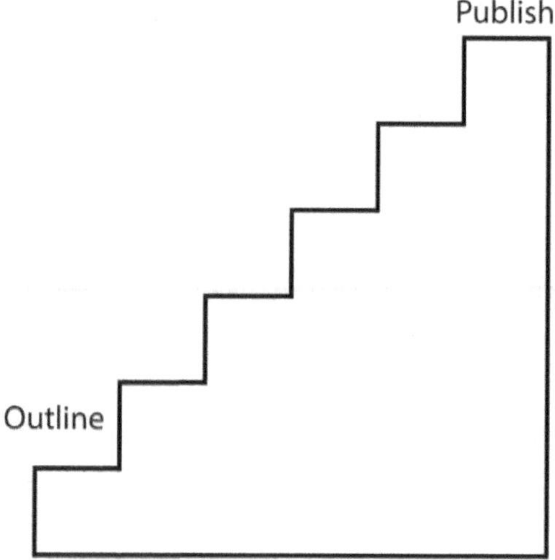

Step 3) Fill in the Intermediate Steps

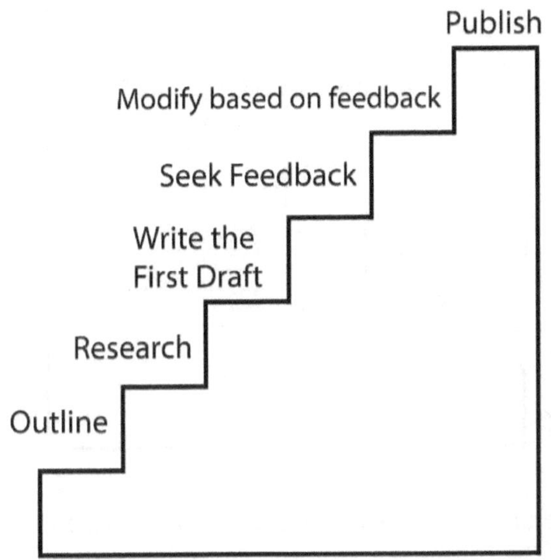

Another example for someone who wants to lose weight but is not sure how to reach their goal can use a staircase like the one shown below:

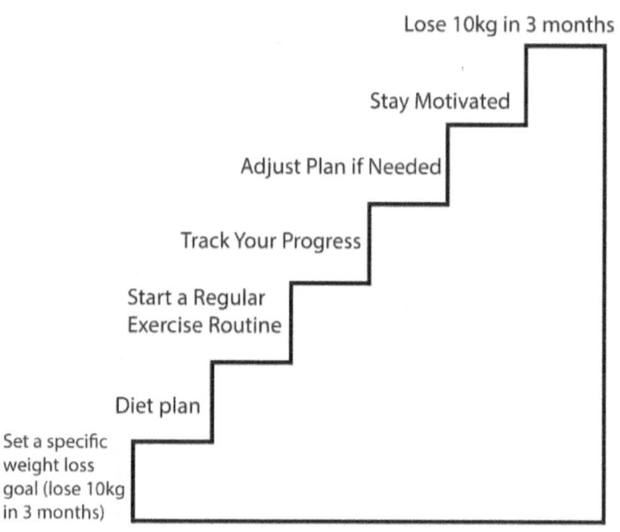

So, I have created my staircase to achieve my goal. I have also made a chart with my goal (created after combining each dimension of SMART) to put on my wall. What goal will you choose to display on your wall? It's time to turn your dreams into visible targets. So, grab your pen and paper—go and make some goals that light up your path and drive you forward.

Chapter 6

Mindfulness — The Power of Now

"Be happy in the moment, that's enough. Each moment is all we need, not more."

~ Mother Teresa

After enlightenment, the Buddha once encountered a man on the road who was mesmerized by his radiant presence. The man, eager to understand the nature of the extraordinary being before him, asked if the Buddha was a god. The Buddha's response was a simple "No." When the man inquired further if he was a wizard or magician, the answer remained "No." Finally, the Buddha replied, "I am awake."

This famous story conveys the essence of mindfulness. The Buddha's response—"I am awake"— summarises a state of deep awareness and clarity that transcends the need for divine labels.

Mindfulness, at its core, is about awakening to the present moment and seeing reality as it truly is, without the distortions of ignorance and illusion. It is about living fully in the here and now, embracing each moment with clarity and understanding.

In the metaphors chapter, we explored various metaphors such as the lighthouse and the eye of the tornado. These images symbolize the self as a non-judging, aware, and constant presence. Mindfulness is precisely this—being fully aware of the present moment without getting entangled in thoughts about "what if," "what could be," or "what will be."

Mindfulness encourages us to anchor ourselves in the now, embracing the current experience without judgment or distraction. It is the practice of observing our thoughts, feelings, and sensations as they arise, without being swept away by them. By cultivating mindfulness, we learn to quiet the non-stop chatter of the mind and find peace in simply being. This practice allows us to respond to life's challenges with clarity and calm, rather than reacting out of habit or fear.

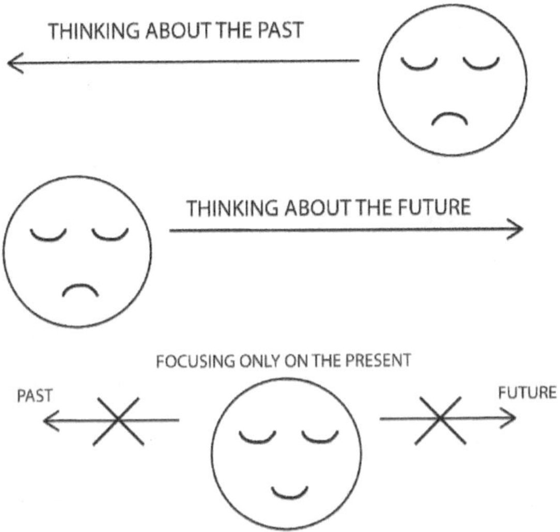

<u>The Unlived Life</u>

Ms. AG was known for her ambition and dedication during her college years. However, her focus was always on the future. Whether she was attending parties, spending time with friends, or even on a college tour, her mind was always occupied with thoughts of upcoming exams, future career prospects, and meticulously planning her next steps. She was present in body but never truly experienced the joy of those moments. While her friends enjoyed the movie nights, experiencing the thrill of each scene, AG was busy planning about what to do next, missing out on the shared laughter and excitement.

After graduation, AG secured a promising job, but her mindset shifted dramatically. Now, her thoughts were dominated by reflections on her college days. She would often find herself pondering about the times she spent with friends, the parties she attended, and the tours she took, filled with a deep sense of regret for not having fully enjoyed those moments. Her focus on the past became a constant source of distraction, preventing her from engaging with her present life and new experiences.

As a result, AG never truly lived in the present. During college, her mind was always in the future, and in her professional life, it was stuck in the past. This inability to be present ruined the true essence of her life—the ability to experience and enjoy each moment as it comes. Her constant concern for what was ahead and what had already passed meant she never fully appreciated or participated in the PRESENT.

Rooted in spiritual traditions, mindfulness is also a growing area of interest in psychology. While a YouTube video by the BBC Channel[1], which I watched a few years ago, doesn't explicitly focus on mindfulness, but beautifully demonstrates its importance. The video showcases the final test for becoming a Shaolin monk. After years of rigorous training, the disciple must attempt a seemingly impossible feat: balancing himself on a free-standing stick, known as a "monkey stick" by Shaolin monks, with his arms outstretched. Despite his training, the disciple initially fails. A Shaolin master then offers a crucial piece of advice to the disciple: to focus on the present moment. This simple instruction highlights the power of mindfulness in achieving even the most challenging tasks.

The tech world has also recently started to acknowledge how notifications and increased digital time are severely affecting people's ability to stay

---

[1] https://www.youtube.com/watch?v=Zbow21FKJS4

present. On Android phones, features like Focus Mode and Do Not Disturb are designed to decrease these adverse impacts to some extent. However, with the rise of smartphones, especially among teenagers, people are not fully living in the present. For example, while watching a scenic view or getting food from a restaurant, the focus often shifts from savouring the moment to taking photos for likes and shares. Even after posting pictures, there is often anticipation for notifications of likes and comments, further moving away from true experience.

Mindfulness in the Palm of Your Hand

Speaking of smartphones, you can start your first mindfulness exercise using your own device. Hold your phone in your hand and take a moment to observe it closely. Notice its size, feel its weight, and examine the color and texture of the back. Pay attention to any scratches or dirt on the screen protector and count the number of camera lenses.

As you do this, thoughts like "I need a new phone" might arise. Acknowledge these thoughts without judgment and gently redirect your focus back to the phone's physical presence. By concentrating on the phone's details, you may find that your worries and distractions begin to fade away. This is because you are not feeding your thoughts with your energy or attention.

This simple exercise illustrates the essence of mindfulness—being fully present with your current experience and observing it without attachment or judgment. Through such practices, you can experience how mindfulness helps in reducing stress and enhancing your ability to stay grounded in the present moment.

Mindful Eyes

Mindfulness through your eyes involves fully engaging with what you see, turning every glance into a moment of appreciation. Look through a window and immerse yourself in the view: the vibrant colors of the sky, the dance of clouds, or the play of light and shadow. Notice the complex details, from the texture of leaves rustling in the breeze to the way sunlight filters through. By observing these visual elements without judgment, you ground yourself in the present moment, savoring the beauty around you. Who knows? Maybe by practicing this mindful observation, you'll find that the next Da Vinci or Shakespeare might just be you, capturing the world's wonders with a new perspective.

Body Scan

Begin by finding a comfortable position, either sitting or lying down. Close your eyes and take a few deep breaths, allowing your body to relax with each exhale.

Start by bringing your attention to your feet. Notice any sensations you might be feeling there, whether warmth, coldness, or contact with the ground. Slowly move your focus up to your ankles, shins, and calves. Observe any areas of tension or relaxation.

Shift your attention to your knees and thighs, feeling the weight of your legs and the sensations in your muscles. Continue moving your awareness up through your hips, pelvis, and lower back. Pay attention to any areas of tightness or ease, without trying to change them.

Next, bring your focus to your abdomen and chest. Notice the rise and fall of your breath, the feeling of your clothing against your skin, and any sensations of relaxation or tension. Move your awareness to your shoulders, arms, and hands. Feel any sensations, like warmth or coolness, and notice if there is any tightness or relaxation.

Finally, bring your attention to your neck, face, and head. Observe the sensations in your scalp, forehead, eyes, and jaw. Notice if there is any tension or ease in these areas.

Take a moment to scan through your entire body, acknowledging any sensations without judgment. As you do this, remind yourself that it's perfectly okay to experience a range of feelings.

Conclude the scan by taking a few more deep breaths. Gently open your eyes when you're ready, bringing your awareness back to the present moment with a sense of calm and connection.

Note: This technique is used in Progressive Muscle Relaxation and is recommended by psychologists for treating a wide range of issues stemming from anxiety.

Tip: Include mindfulness in your timetable, especially in the leisure domain.

Metaphors and Mindfulness

Psychology is not merely a science of following predetermined steps to reach a conclusion; rather, it is an art form, similar to cooking, where various techniques and ingredients can be combined to enhance the overall experience. Just as a chef blends flavours to create a unique dish, so too can we blend psychological techniques to enrich our understanding and practice. One intriguing fusion is the integration of mindfulness and metaphor.

Mindfulness and metaphors are powerful tools that, when integrated, can significantly enrich our practice and understanding. Mindfulness is the practice of being fully present and engaged in the moment, while metaphors are symbolic representations that can help us conceptualize complex ideas and experiences. By combining these two, we can deepen our mindfulness practice and gain a more profound insight into our internal and external worlds.

Creating Metaphors through Mindfulness:

Mindfulness can facilitate the creation of metaphors by encouraging a deep observation of our thoughts, feelings, and surroundings. As we become more in harmony with our present experience, we may naturally begin to see patterns or connections that can be expressed metaphorically. For instance, if we notice that our mind feels like a turbulent sea, we might use the metaphor of "navigating stormy waters" to describe our emotional state. This metaphor helps encapsulate the essence of our experience in a way that is both vivid and accessible.

Enhancing Mindfulness through Metaphors:

Conversely, metaphors can enhance mindfulness by providing us with relatable imagery to anchor our attention. For example, the metaphor of a "calm lake" can be used during mindfulness practice to help visualize a state of inner tranquility. By focusing on this metaphor, we create a mental image that represents the peacefulness we aim to cultivate. Similarly, the metaphor of "leaves floating on a stream" can be used to represent letting go of intrusive thoughts, helping practitioners to observe their thoughts without getting caught up in them.

Integrating Metaphors into Mindfulness Practice:

To integrate metaphors into your mindfulness practice, you can begin by choosing metaphors that resonate with your current emotional state or goals. During meditation or mindful reflection, visualize or contemplate these metaphors to guide your focus. For instance, if you're dealing with stress, imagine yourself as a "mountain" that remains steady and unmoved despite the "storm" around you. This can help ground your practice and provide a sense of stability and strength.

Another approach is to use metaphors in mindfulness exercises, such as body scans or mindful breathing. For example, you might imagine your breath as "waves" gently washing over the shore, helping you to focus on the rhythm and flow of your breath. Similarly, during a body scan, visualize each muscle group as "softening like wax" to facilitate relaxation.

By merging metaphors into your mindfulness practice, you create a richer experience that can enhance both your understanding and application of mindfulness. This integration allows for a more creative and personalized approach, making mindfulness practice more engaging and impactful.

Chapter 7

Unconscious — Be Whole, Not Just a Good Part

"How can I be substantial if I do not cast a shadow? I must have a dark side also if I am to be whole."

~ Carl Jung

Neither this book nor a person can be complete without acknowledging the unconscious. The mind can be broadly divided into two main parts: the conscious and the unconscious. The conscious mind includes thoughts and feelings that we are currently aware of and can actively think about or control. This includes our immediate perceptions, decisions, and deliberate actions. In contrast, the unconscious mind contains thoughts, memories, and desires that lie outside our immediate awareness but still influence our behavior and emotions. It includes repressed experiences such as trauma from childhood that remains buried in the unconscious, hidden fears like a deep-seated anxiety, and unacknowledged desires, such as suppressed sexual fantasies or desires that are not openly admitted.

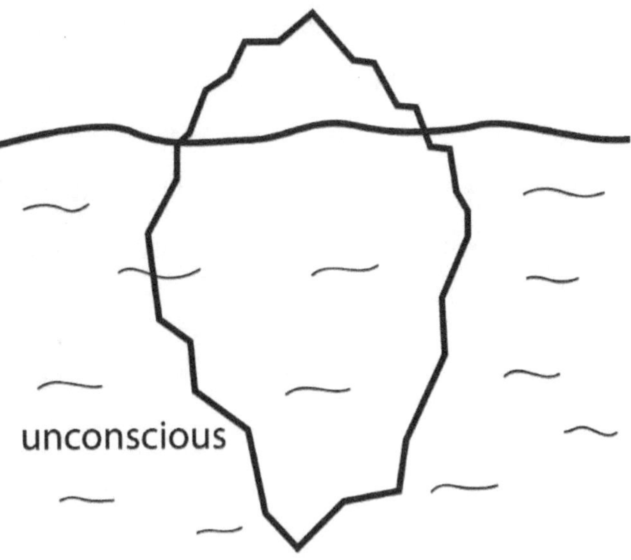

When Sigmund Freud and Carl Jung first met in Vienna, their conversation lasted an astonishing 13 hours without a break—truly an impressive conversation that could put even the most talkative lovers to shame! Their initial meeting was marked by a deep intellectual connection and shared enthusiasm for exploring the depths of the human mind. However, as they explored further into the complexities of the unconscious, their paths began to diverge. Freud had introduced the ground-breaking concept of the unconscious, laying the groundwork for future explorations. Jung, inspired by Freud's ideas, expanded upon them, but his work soon began to blur the line between mysticism and science. This shift did not sit well with Freud, who criticized Jung's increasingly mysterious theories one's conscious identity.

Freud primarily viewed the unconscious as a storehouse of repressed sexual and aggressive impulses. It was largely seen as a negative force that needed to be controlled.

Unconscious — The Shadow You Hate

Imagine the unconscious as the shadow you hate. Often depicted as a figure longing for acceptance and recognition, the unconscious is consistently pushed away. It stays persistently, following us through life like a constant, though often unwelcome, presence. This metaphor captures the essence of the unconscious's complex relationship with us. One that is frequently denied and repressed but remains an inseparable part of our mind. Despite our efforts to ignore or distance ourselves from it, the unconscious continues to seek acknowledgment.

However, the unconscious is an intrinsic part of you, deeply rooted in your psyche. Unlike an abandoned lover, the shadow cannot be discarded or forgotten. It possesses deep knowledge of your inner world, aware of aspects of yourself that you have yet to discover. The unconscious is not a passive entity that will quietly accept your rejection. It demands acknowledgment; it will ensure its existence is recognized, its voice is heard. Embracing this shadow, rather than hating it, is essential for achieving wholeness and integrating all parts of your being.

"No tree, it is said, can grow to heaven unless its roots reach down to hell."

~ Carl Jung

Carl Jung's quote above emphasises the necessity of acknowledging and integrating our unconscious aspects to attain wholeness. We often prioritize becoming "good" people, unconsciously neglecting the cultivation of our entire selves. The true aim of our psychological journey is to embrace our totality, flaws and strengths alike.

This growth is not without its challenges. It requires confronting the demons within, a process that can be painful and unsettling. However, it's exactly through these trials that we cultivate resilience and depth. The more we understand and accept our unconscious aspects, the more we expand our consciousness and evolve into fully realized individuals.

Person A

Appears kind, polite, and morally upright to others. Focuses on maintaining a positive public image, often at the expense of personal authenticity.

Person A has always avoided confronting his unconscious; hence, it comes to the surface in unpredictable ways, such as:

- Unresolved fears, desires, and emotions
- Increased Internal Conflict
- Relationship issues

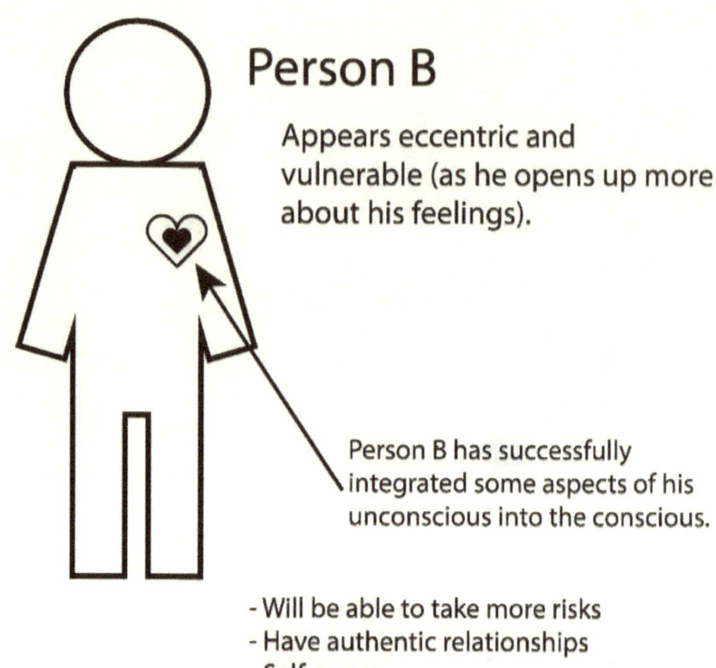

This perspective challenges traditional parenting and societal rules that often prioritize goodness over wholeness. We are frequently conditioned to suppress our darker impulses and emotions in favour of presenting a socially acceptable face ☺ It is unfortunate that the effects of this forced conformity were not fully understood in the past. Such suppression can lead to a host of issues later in life, including low self-esteem, anxiety, and depression.

"Unexpressed emotions will never die. They are buried alive and will come forth later in uglier ways."

~ Sigmund Freud

Freud recognized the significance of the unconscious mind and its influence on conscious behavior. He said that if these unconscious elements remain unaddressed, they can manifest in unpredictable ways. Much like an iceberg, the majority of our mental processes lie beneath the surface, exerting a powerful influence on our thoughts, feelings, and actions. By neglecting to explore and understand our unconscious, we risk allowing these hidden forces to control us rather than the other way around.

Integrating Unconscious into Conscious

Exploring and integrating the unconscious is a complex process that this brief book can only touch on. Often, it requires the guidance of a therapist for a deeper exploration.

Sublimation

Introduced by Sigmund Freud. Sublimation involves channeling the energy and desires from the unconscious into constructive and socially acceptable activities. Some examples are

- <u>Unconscious Aggressive Impulse</u> → <u>Boxing</u>

For example, consider Mr. JG, who has aggressive impulses residing in his unconscious. Instead of allowing these impulses to disrupt his daily life or relationships, he channels this energy into competitive sports. By engaging in activities like boxing, Mr. JG finds a productive outlet for his aggression, which helps him maintain balance and improve his overall well-being. This process not only helps in managing his unconscious desires but also promotes personal growth and positive self-expression.

- <u>Unconscious Sexual Impulses</u> → <u>Art</u>

Ms. AS, a talented artist, grapples with unconscious sexual impulses that she finds socially unacceptable. To channel this energy constructively, she sublimates these desires into her artwork. Her paintings, often characterized by bold colors and sensual forms, serve as an outlet for her repressed sexuality. By transforming these raw impulses into creative expression, Ms. AS not only finds personal fulfillment but also produces art that resonates with others.

- <u>Unconscious Fear</u> → <u>Curiosity</u>

Mr. U grapples with unconscious fear of ghosts. To manage this anxiety, he turns his attention to parapsychology, the study of paranormal phenomena. By immersing himself in research and investigation of the unexplained, Mr. U transforms his fear into curiosity. This academic pursuit allows him to confront his phobia in a controlled, rational manner and thus gradually reducing its grip on his mind.

Mindfulness

Mindfulness is an excellent way to connect your unconscious mind with your conscious awareness. By focusing on the present and observing your thoughts, feelings, and physical sensations without judgment, you create a space for hidden parts of yourself to emerge. With regular mindfulness practice, you'll start to see patterns that highlight repressed desires, hidden fears, and unresolved conflicts. This compassionate, non-judgmental approach allows you to bring these unconscious elements to light, making them easier to understand and accept. Over time, this helps you achieve better emotional balance, self-awareness, and a greater sense of wholeness.

It has been a privilege talking to you. <3